I0053727

THE SECRET GUIDE TO MAKING MONEY WITH INVESTMENTS

LEARN WHAT TO INVEST IN & HAVE YOUR MONEY WORK FOR YOU

TODD WILLIAMS

CONTENTS

INTRODUCTION

This book contains proven steps and strategies on how to consistently make a passive income by investing. It's about growing your money the smart and easy way possible. It includes a range from safe methods to risky investments.

Throw away the get-rich quick schemes that never work and turn off the financial news because it's constant noise. Whether your dream is protecting your assets in a turbulent market or growing your wealth so that you can retire in style, this book is the blueprint to your financial success.

Let's begin.

DOUBLING YOUR MONEY EVERY 7-10 YEARS

D id you know that if you leave your money untouched in any solidly proven, dividend earning, non-speculative investment portfolio you can be almost sure that it will eventually double in value over a certain period of time? It is a mathematical probability that use the power of compounding interest. Investment bankers and brokers have had this knowledge for a long time. They call it the infamous Rule of 72.

The Rule of 72 is basically a mathematical shortcut meant to determine the future value of a certain amount. Specifically, it calculates the length of time it will take an investment to double in value if it is left to grow with compounding interest. According to the rule, if you divide the number 72 by the annual rate of return it will give you the length of time for your money to double with the given rate.

MATHEMATICALLY, the Rule of 72 is expressed as follows:

Annual Rate multiplied by Number of Years (for it to double) = 72

If the annual rate is given, you can get the Number of Years (for it to double) with this:

Number of Years (for it to double) = 72 divided by the given Annual Rate

If you want to know at the rate you will double your money for a given number of years you can use this:

Annual Rate = 72 divided by desired Number of Years

FOLLOWING THE FORMULA ABOVE, you will arrive at 7.2 years for your money to double its value at 10% compounded annual rate of return (72/10%). Similarly, you can calculate that it will take 10 years for your money to double at 7.2% (72/7.2).

Clearly the ball is really on your side of the court. As indicated by the calculations above, it is highly possible for you to double your money within 7 to 10 years - but for that to happen you need to invest your money in a portfolio mix that gives an annual collective yield of between 7.2% and 10% c. Using this as your basis therefore, what you need to do is to carefully put together a mix of investment instruments which have demonstrated their consistency in providing similar yields in the past. The bottom line is - it still is your call.

Your choices of where to put your money will actually

depend a lot on what kind of an investor you are - as well as on your appetite for taking risks.

If you are the conservative kind with no appetite for risk taking then your portfolio must only include investments which are considered relatively safe and stable. This can be a diversified mixture of blue chip stocks and investment grade bonds.

Blue chip stocks are those issued by financially stable and well-established companies with billions of dollars in capitalization. These companies are not likely to go under in the near term. They are also known for paying increasing dividends through the years (some even for decades).

On the other hand, investment grade bonds are municipal or corporate bonds with high (AAA to AA) to medium (A to BBB) credit rating and are therefore thought to be least likely to default.

Let's assume that you have a portfolio mix made up evenly of blue chips stocks and investment grade bonds. If the blue-chip stocks in your portfolio have an average annual yield of 10% and your investment grade bonds have an annual return of roughly 6%, then these two should collectively give you a net return of 8%. Using the Rule of 72 formula, you divide 72 by the net return (8%) to get 9 years - the length of time to keep your money invested in this mix for it to double its value - and 18 years to quadruple it.

The speculative investors may however find the waiting time of 7 to 10 years too long and too boring. They are the types of investors who are willing to face bigger risks for bigger pay-offs. They are fully aware of the fact that in investing, the bigger the risks you take, the bigger the rewards will be. And because they are in a hurry to super-size the value of their investments, they prefer to put their money on the more volatile stock options, delve on highly leveraged trading, or get engrossed with picking penny stocks. These are the type of investment where you can double your money overnight or lose your shirt just as fast.

SOME WORDS OF CAUTION THOUGH. If it's a nest egg you want to build for the future which you are looking forward to helping you go through your golden years comfortably, then it's best to avoid being speculative. Set your sights instead on placements that will provide you with reasonable and stable annual returns with less risk.

And in case somebody comes along trying to convince you to join their speculative bandwagon by showing you his almost spotless trading records, put one thing in your mind – "A sterling performance in the past is not a guarantee of future results." Resist the temptation to turbo-charge your investments and stay conservative. Your money is bound to eventually double in time anyway so why take the extra risks?

BELOW IS a Rule of 72 chart showing the type of returns that will double your money over a corresponding period of time. This may help you in your search for the best placements for your money that will double it in time.

% Annual Investment Yield

Number of Years to Double your Money

2

WHY MOST INVESTORS ACHIEVE
STUNNINGLY POOR RETURNS

I t's no big secret that most investors achieve stunningly poor returns on their money. Some of them even end up with drastically impaired capital while a significant number lose theirs completely. Obviously, there is something they are not doing right. One of most foreboding thing about investing is every mistake you make can drastically impact investment returns and may even lead to a significant loss of your capital.

Therefore, it will definitely help you a great deal to know exactly what these investors are doing wrong so you can avoid falling in the same dire investing predicaments.

Getting started, here are some of the many mistakes most investors commit:

Investing **without an investment strategy or plan**

Any form of investment can be likened to journeying through rough seas. An investment strategy is what serves as your navigational map which will guide you in reaching your destination. Without such a map, it may be impossible

to cross the 'rough seas' (the market) and reach your destination (your investment objectives). You may end up some-
where else you don't want to be.

INVESTING for a living or with a "Paycheck Mentality"

It will be disastrous to start investing hoping you'll earn
enough to replace your paycheck. Many have tried doing it
by becoming day traders. It forces you to engage in short
term plays - buying and selling stocks feverishly in an
attempt to make small gains from short term price movements. Unfortunately getting in and out of the market more
frequently comes at a stiff price – the outlandish fees you
have to pay your brokers and the higher risk exposure.
Besides, it is very rare for short term players to outperform
the market. And if ever they do, they still end up underper-
forming once you deduct the aggregate brokers' fees that
pile up.

What you need is a long-term plan particularly if your
portfolio is meant to tidy you up during your golden years.
As one successful investor once said "you must treat your
investment decisions as if you only have 15 trades to make
throughout the life span of each investment".

PUTTING ALL your Eggs in One basket by failing to diversify

Many investors tend to put all their money on stocks of
companies belonging to the same industry. Such a move is
quite risky because if anything adverse happens the whole
portfolio will go down with it. The best thing to do is to thin
out your risk exposure by broadly diversifying your holdings – spreading your money on different asset classes and

not just on one. It is also important to strike a balance in your holdings such that you achieve maximum gains with the less risks.

INVESTING in stocks without doing due diligence on the company

Many investors invest in stocks because they simply like it or in a spur of the moment thought perhaps influenced by the stock's most recent favorable price movements without doing some due diligence work or without assessing the company's financial standing and its profit potential in the long term.

Making a stock or a bond pick out of whims or without careful evaluation is a perfect formula for disaster.

TOO MUCH ATTENTION on Media broadcasted Financial Advice

Stock or bond picks taken from financial news shows will not really help you achieve your goals. They are mostly done with hindsight. If you reflect on the wisdom of it, do you think anyone who has a profitable investment tip or a secret formula will announce it on live television? For sure, they would rather keep it to themselves and make their millions than continue making a living blabbering in the boob tube or publishing financial newsletter with investing tips.

BUYING HIGH, Selling Low

People often try to jump in or out of a bandwagon too late. They observe the rise of rallying stocks with guarded caution and only make their decision to buy after it's ready to peak. Or, they hold on to 'losers' too long in the hope that they will bounce back so they can at least break even only to dispose them at a bigger loss after realizing too late that the slide is bound to continue. As a result, they either buy high or sell low which is contrary to the main trading dictum which is to buy low and sell high.

SHORT TERM MARKET Movements

Almost all investors try to time their entry into or exit from a trade by predicting short term market movements. They are more often than not - always wrong. The best way is to evaluate the long term potential of a security to make profits then buy and hold.

GOING the way of the high-frequency traders

High frequency traders buy and sell securities more often than they change their under wears. No less than investing icon Warren Buffet warned us against this when he said you are making a big mistake if you are trading actively. He is a firm believer in buying and holding a security for the long haul.

UNMINDFUL OF FEES and expenses they have to shell

A lot of investors prefer to park their money on large, well established mutual funds unmindful of the expensive management fees that goes with it. However, Warren Buffett thinks you are making a big mistake "if you are incurring large expenses in connection with your investing you are making a big mistake". And Buffett has every reason to caution us with this warning. In the first place there are low-cost index funds that are almost replicates large mutual funds so why go for one which entails bigger costs on your end?

TRADING WITH BORROWED **Money**

Trading with borrowed money makes a nervous trader out of you. You tend to cash in early and allow your losses to run. As proof of this, statistics show that 3 out of 4 fortunes lost in trading are from accounts traded with borrowed money.

Too **proud to admit mistakes**

A lot of traders develop a wrong notion that the market will move in the direction pointed to by their exhaustive market analysis. They become too stubborn to make adjustments in their strategies even in the face of a rapidly changing market conditions. They often overestimate their trading prowess and toadmit their mistakes much less recognize them.

are too proud Over and over again, studies show that we substantially overestimate our own investment capabilities and our performance relative to the market. And we don't like to recognize and acknowledge our mistakes—even to ourselves. Too often, we are also stubborn. Remember the adage: "The stock doesn't know you own it." And it really doesn't care about you.

HASTILY TRADING ON 'TIPS'

Many investors have developed the habit of trading

breaking news. They are also gullible for "insider tips".
While this may work at times, more often than not it brings
negative results. The best way is not to rely on tips or
depend on breaking news to initiate a trade. Instead, do an
exhaustive and market analysis and use it as the basis of
your trades.

HAVING the Herd Mentality

Most traders have ingrained the herd mentality into
their trading style – buying a security after seeing a mob of
traders chalking up a particular security and are quick to
bailout when they everyone else selling them. This trading
style is akin to 'buying high, selling low' where too often
investors find themselves buying at the top of a rally and
selling at the trough of a bear market.

It is not wise to call 'all in' just because everybody else is
buying up a "hot" asset. It is the best way to get burned.

BUYING a security you have very little understanding of

Buying in into a security whose potential risk and
rewards you hardly understand or at worst know nothing of
is tantamount to gambling. Many investors commit this
mistake only to regret miserably afterwards. This happens a
lot especially if you have the habit of following other people
in their trades. The prudent way is to investigate and understand the potential risks and rewards of a security before
committing your money to it.

BEING an emotional trader

Investors trading without a clear cut investment strategy

rely a lot on their gut feel and trade with their emotions. It's the gut not the brains which leads them to initiate a trade. Often, they become emotional particularly when nursing a losing investment. They tend to hang on to it in the hope that prices will rebound enough for them to get out even. But when the market does turn in their favor way, they abandon thoughts of breaking even and hang on thinking that they were right all along. And when the market resumes its negative course, they are reduced to nervous wrecks looking for a way to bail out – too late.

3

OUT-PERFORM THE MAJORITY OF PROFESSIONAL INVESTORS WHILE TAKING LESS RISK

The vast majority of professional investors have adapted a shorter term view of the market for a long time - looking for earning opportunities in what they view as an inefficient market. Believing that the market is not always able to immediately factor into the price all relevant information, they actively search for undervalued securities to purchase. They hope to make a profit when the prices of the undervalued securities finally settle down to their real fair market values – which may or may not happen. They try to capitalize on short term price movements squeezing in and out of the volatile market - buying and selling what they view as undervalued securities with uncanny frequency.

In short, the vast majority of professional investors have a short-sighted view of the market actively chasing perceived investing opportunities and timing their trades with the use of self-serving technical analysis tools with the aim of outperforming the market.

Their view of the market as inefficient is in stark contrast to the well founded theory on efficient markets - which states that the market always factors in to the price all relevant information about the security as they happen and when they happen – without delay. This means securities are always valued correctly and will never be undervalued or overvalued based on existing fundamentals and other relevant information underlying the particular securities. To view a security as undervalued or overvalued in relation to a perceived future fair value is therefore merely speculative and unfounded. This is why the performance of most of these professional investors who actively manage their investments always falls way below actual market returns.

Despite the fact that only a little over 20% of them are able to outperform the corresponding market indexes while the rest miserably lag the market, professional investors stubbornly stick to their investing strategy and continue to actively trade their accounts, time the market, and search for perceived undervalued assets.

The best way to outperform them therefore is to do the exact opposite of what they are doing - have a good, long-term strategy – one that will remain resilient during bad times and at the same time able to cash in during good times.

BUILDING long term strategies

Long term investing strategies entails putting together a mix of the less risky and less volatile securities which most investors normally shy away from because of what they view as their laggard performance. Long term strategies may take time and may require a great deal of your patience before it starts to deliver the desired results. However, over time, they will be able to deliver better returns than the more volatile securities which active traders are typically fond of.

Studies made by Russell Investments showed that the more volatile securities (those with higher Betas) produced lower returns than the less risky, less volatile securities over time. Apparently the trading axiom 'less risk, less reward' no longer holds water here - particularly with securities long time traders call as Dividend Aristocrats (securities that have continually raised their yearly dividends for the last 25 years).

The study cites Pepsico as an example of a Dividend Aristocrat which has a low risk factor (low beta) yet provides high returns to its shareholders. Pepsico is up 25% over the last year. It has an average 5 year dividend growth rate of 6.25% which makes it ideal for the long haul. ConAgra Foods is another example which is up 16% over the last year.

There are other small cap, low risk, high reward securities too like IdaCorp. You must however hold on to these stocks long term for you to gain the biggest payback from the rising share prices. Over time, the pay-off from this long term strategy will far exceed the performance of the vast majority of professional traders.

QUICKLY SETUP A PORTFOLIO OF DIVERSIFIED EXCHANGE TRADED FUNDS (ETFS)

One of the best ways to minimize the risk of investing is to spread your capital exposure thinly to as many different securities representing various asset classes as possible. This way, if anything adverse happens to a particular asset class, the rest of your holdings will remain unaffected and keep you afloat and out of the red. Unfortunately, this entails putting together a portfolio of at least about 50 to100 securities from different asset classes. Admittedly, this is a tall order for an individual investor to tackle all by himself.

Fortunately, there is now the ETF or Exchange Trade Fund which consists of a basket of securities similar to an index fund which tracks the price movement of that particular index. It is traded much like the way stocks are traded with its price fluctuating throughout the day as it is bought and sold in an exchange.

ETFs provide instant diversification. A single ETF share gives you ownership to a basket of securities – definitely better than buying a single share of a stock. It also costs less to put your money on ETFs than to buy into a mutual fund (which we know entails excessive management fees).

How do you build a diversified ETF portfolio?

THE QUICKEST WAY TO build a portfolio of ETFs that is well diversified is to go for low cost, index based ETFs. You can actually start one with just 3 cheap ETFs with three major asset components namely domestic equities, international equities, and bonds. An example of this 3 ETF strategy is shown below:

- VTI (Vanguard Total Stock Market Index) for domestic equities
- VXUS (Vanguard Total International Stock) for international equities
- BND (Vanguard Total Bond Market) for the bond component

All three has less than 1% expense ratios each and gives you exposure to more than 15,000 stock and bond issues altogether.

There are other low cost funds you can combine together to form a diversified ETF portfolio similar to Vanguard's above. You can form your cheap 3 ETF strategy from Black Rock's:

- ITOT (iShares Core S&P Total U.S. Stock Market)
- IXUS (iShares Core MSCI Total International Stock)

- AGG (iShares Core Total U.S. Bond Market).

Similarly, all three also have less than 1% expense ratio each. However, this iShare 3 ETF strategy from Black Rock provides you with an exposure to only 6,700 stock and bond component. It would be a good starting point though to get you started with very minimal capital exposure.

An alternative approach to the 3 ETF strategies outlined above is to pick:

- One global stock ETF
- One global bond ETF
- 5 % to 10% alternative assets such as real estate or commodities.

Limiting your ETF portfolio to just 3 ETFs for a start is not only going to be cost effective but will deliver substantial yield and balanced risks. And, as you gain more confidence and experience you'd be able to rebalance your portfolio to shape your holdings to fit your specific time frame, your risk appetite, and targeted earnings in the future.

PUT IN 3 TO 5 HOURS A YEAR, AND OUT-PERFORM 80% OF INVESTORS

I t may sound improvable but it is definitely possible - you can beat 80% of investors while trading only 3 to 5 hours a year. The simple strategy you can use to achieve this is called passive investing. Some describe this investing strategy as a 'couch potato strategy' since it essentially involves buying and holding securities for the long term.

'Passive Investing' is in essence index investing where buying a share of the index fund allows you to own a broad spectrum of securities representative of various asset classes. It allows you to capture the returns of the whole market which means it doesn't matter if one or several securities are lagging the market. What matters is making money over time from the collective return of all the assets that were pooled together into the index fund. All you need to do after carefully selecting your basket of securities that will make up your passive investment portfolio is to just leave them there to appreciate in value through the years.

But make no mistake about it because it is definitely not

a 'set it and forget it' kind of thing. You need to review your portfolio regularly within a year to make sure the original weight you gave each asset class security remains the same. Changing market conditions may necessitate rebalancing your portfolio which should take at least 3 to 5 hours each year.

So, how does this beat 80% of investors?

As discussed in an earlier chapter of this book the vast majority of investors (80%) are actively managing their investments. They believe the market is inefficient and it does not immediately factor every market development into the price. That is why they are in constant search for under-valued securities so they can gain from possible short term price movements. In other words, they are timing the market hoping to generate better than market returns.

For varying reasons, these unfortunate investors have stubbornly stuck to their habit of constantly searching for undervalued securities and continue timing the markets. Sadly, history has always proven them wrong as evidenced by the fact that the returns they manage to get consistently lag the market year after year after year. Only about a little over 20% of them managed to beat the market occasionally.

It would then be easy to outperform the vast majority of these investors who actively manage their investments. How? By being a 'couch potato' investor - by taking the opposing view and going long term. This is exactly what passive investingt is all about.

Passive investing (in contrast to active investing) is founded on the theory that the market is efficient. It factors all and every market development into the price without delay. This means there is no way a security will be under-valued or overvalued at any given time as current prices already reflect the security's fair value. Over time a security is bound to accumulate value This puts to rest the argument of an inefficient market which all active investors adhere to – in short there is no more need to actively buy and sell securities.

There are three main benefits of passive investing:

- It provides near-market returns.
- It makes portfolio diversification easy.
- It costs less than any active investing strategy.

As the securities market gets more and more efficient information wise with the advent of new technologies, active investors will find it more difficult to make money. Passive investing on the other hand can be expected to continue outperforming active investing over time. Meanwhile stock picking will slowly become a thing of the past.

WHY WON'T the most popular index mutual funds result in a properly diversified portfolio?

IF YOU ARE THINKING that because you own several of the most popular index mutual funds, your investment portfolio is already properly diversified, you may be in for some rude re-awakening. Having several funds in your portfolio mix is not a guarantee that you have covered all the bases. If fact, it may result in fund overlaps which can effectively reduce the benefits of diversification.

Fund overlaps results from having two or more funds which have positions in the same securities. This can kneecap your entire investment portfolio especially if those same securities present in two or more of your funds suffer a negative loss. In other words, it unnecessarily exposes you to greater risks since you are holding on to more of the same kind of security. It negates the primary reason why you need to diversify – which is to have adequate downside protection. It protects your portfolio from going under in case one sector goes haywire and delivers poor performance. Having fund overlaps also mean part of your capital is unnecessarily tied to the same security effectively limiting your upward exposure.

Having fund overlaps is unavoidable particularly if you obtain different funds from different companies with different managers. Each one of these fund managers is likely to include the most popular and most profitable security in their respective mixes causing a fund overlap if you include them in your portfolio mix. Small amounts of overlaps are tolerable. However, extreme overlaps can turn your portfolio into a lame duck.

WHAT YOU NEED TO DO...

There is no easy way to check for overlaps. The best thing to do is to check each fund every quarter and compare the top holdings of each fund with one another. If two or more of the funds have overweighted the same security then you may consider retaining only one of the funds and replacing the other (or others) with another fund (or funds). Checking for overlaps in your mutual fund holdings can be difficult and tedious. You can pay for a service to check for overlaps or you can manually analyze and compare the top holdings of each of your funds.

It is easier though to avoid overlaps if you are just starting your investment portfolio. The secret is to choose funds with different objectives. That way, you can be almost sure that there won't be an overlap in their top holdings.

THE PROMISES OF ENDOWMENTS & MUTUAL FUNDS

P rior to 1987, money held by the Yale University Endowment used to be invested in just two classes of assets – Domestic Equities and fixed income. When David Swensen took over as chief investment officer in 1987, he pursued a more aggressive investment strategy expanding his placements beyond the conventional norm into the realm of the non-traditional, illiquid assets like private equity, real estate, foreign equity, and absolute return.

His foresight paid off as he racked 20 straight years of positive growth which saw the Yale Endowment balloon from $1 billion to $17b. His unconventional strategy became the investment model of other mammoth endowments as they attempted to duplicate what he did. What he did was well studied, copied, yet never equaled.

The key elements of his pragmatic and innovative approach to investing include:

- Multi-asset investing (Diversification of portfolio)

- Strategic asset allocation, (Maximizing Risk Adjusted Returns)
- And inclusion of alternative asset classes into the mix.

Individual investors may not have access to the same superior resources David Swensen had in his command but certainly they can apply the same principles to achieve risk adjusted returns that are more superior than those of the traditional portfolios.

For example, in terms of multi-asset investing, you can apply the same principles in your selection of index based funds or ETFs.

In terms of strategic asset allocation for individual port-folios, Swensen recommends a bigger allocation to domestic equities (30%), followed by REITs (20%), Foreign Equities (15%), Bonds (15%), TIPS (15%), and Emerging Markets (5%). Strategic asset allocation is the most important aspect of the Yale endowment model. It provides you the flexibility to pool together different asset classes that not only maximize your risk adjusted returns but also outperform other portfolios.

WHY DO a considerable number of mutual funds fail to live up to their promise?

According to the book "Common Sense on Mutual Funds" written by John C. Boggle who did extensive analyses of mutual funds only 1 out of 7 mutual funds can beat the market in 25 years. He said the number goes down to 1 out of 20 if you are talking about outperforming the market by at least 1 %. What this simply means is if you put your money on a mutual fund you are 7 times more likely to lose money relative to the market index.

The bottom line is the vast majority of mutual funds simply fail to live up to their promise year after year after year. And they have ventured tons of explanation for this – from simply picking the wrong stocks, or picking profitable stocks but the income is not good enough to cover the cost of the fund. Other reasons range from dubious management to being overly diversified which along with the horrendous management fees they charge erodes whatever returns the fund is able to generate for the investors.

Apart from the reasons mentioned above, there are four other explanations why mutual funds are doomed from the start.

- First, it is actively managed and the managers are placed in a dire position where they have to outwit the powerful force of an efficient market. But, as the market becomes more and more efficient aided by the influx of new technologies, it has become harder for these managers to find undervalued securities they can make money on.
- Second, stocks today have a tendency to move in correlation with each other moved by broader economic forces. This makes it even more difficult for fund managers to do their stock picking.
- Third, because of regulations that govern mutual funds in the U.S. which limits the money they can invest in any company, their upside growth potential is effectively watered down. Any upward growth can only happen at a slower pace.

- Fourth, the horrendously high management fees and other hidden costs normally charged by mutual fund companies tend to eat up whatever returns the fund may have gained for the investors. As a result, it is the fund managers and not the investors who really rake in the biggest gains – unfortunately at the expense of their investors.

AFTERWORD

I hope this was an eye-opener for you in many ways. I hope you have a clearer picture on how to get started with investing as well as build a strong portfolio so that you can make a profitable and good living for many years to come.

www.ingramcontent.com/pod-product-compliance
Lightning Source LLC
Chambersburg PA
CBHW071533210326
41597CB00018B/2982